SCHOLAS
New
Nonfiction Reaaers®

MW00943103

This Is the Way We Play

By Amanda Miller

Children's Press®
An Imprint of Scholastic Inc.
New York Toronto London Auckland Sydney
Mexico City New Delhi Hong Kong
Danbury, Connecticut

These content vocabulary word builders are for grades 1–2.

Subject Consultant: Eli J. Lesser, MA, Director of Education, National Constitution Center, Philadelphia, Pennsylvania

Reading Consultant: Cecilia Minden-Cupp, PhD, Early Literacy Consultant and Author, Chapel Hill, North Carolina

Photographs © 2010: Alamy Images: back cover, 9, 21 left center (Arco Images GmbH), 16 (Eye Ubiquitous), 11, 20 left (Hemis), 2, 15, 20 right center (JupiterImages/BananaStock), 1, 19, 21 right (Friedrich Stark), 17, 20 right (Ariadne Van Zandbergen); Corbis Images: 13 bottom, 21 left (David Bathgate), 13 top (Syed Jan Sabawoon/epa); Getty Images: cover (B-C Images), 5 bottom right (Donna Day), 5 top left (Lawrence Migdale), 5 top right, 21 right center (Dave Nagel), 7, 20 left center (Bob Thomas); iStockphoto: 18, 22 top (Ivan Bajic), 6 (Larysa Dodz), 14, 23 top (kemie), 10, 23 bottom (Michaela Kindle), 12, 22 bottom (Jonathan Larsen), 8 (luxxtek); Viesti Associates, Inc./Bill Bachmann: 5 bottom left.
Map 20-21: Jim McMahon

Art Direction and Production: Scholastic Classroom Magazines

Library of Congress Cataloging-in-Publication Data

Miller, Amanda.
This is the way we play / Amanda Miller.
    p. cm.
Includes bibliographical references and index.
ISBN 13: 978-0-531-21342-1 (lib. bdg.) 978-0-531-21442-8 (pbk.)
ISBN 10: 0-531-21342-0 (lib. bdg.) 0-531-21442-7 (pbk.)
1. Play–Juvenile literature. 2. Games–Juvenile literature. I. Title.
GV182.9.M55 2009   790.1'922–dc22 2009010973

CONTENTS

Do You Play With Your Friends?

What games do you like to play? Do you have a favorite toy?

Kids around the world play in many ways. Let's see how they play!

These children play in the United States.

Sports

These boys love to chase a **soccer ball**! They live near the ocean so they play soccer right on the beach. Sometimes they play in their bare feet!

soccer ball

These boys play soccer in Brazil.

These kids play a sport called cricket. They have to hit a small ball with a flat **bat**. The ball goes high in the air!

bat

These children play cricket in Australia.

Toys

These girls play with wooden **tops** called *koma*. The tops spin on sticks. The girls keep the tops spinning as long as they can.

tops

These girls spin tops in Japan.

These kids love windy days. Why? They get to fly **kites**!

Here, men and boys often fly kites together. On some days the sky is filled with kites!

kites

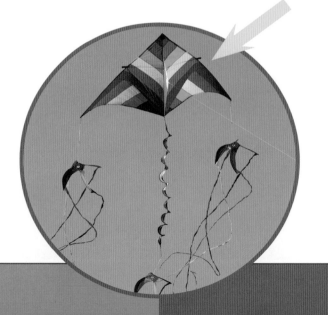

These boys fly kites in Afghanistan.

13

Games

This boy plays a game of **marbles**. He shoots the marble with his thumb! He tries to knock the other player's marbles out of the game.

marbles

This boy plays marbles in England.

These girls play **mancala**. The game pieces are rocks. The board has cups in it.

If children don't have a board, that's OK. They just dig holes in the sand.

mancala

These girls play mancala in Kenya.

17

These sisters play **jump rope** games. They sing or count as they jump. Each time they start to jump, they try to jump more times than the last!

What do *you* like to play?

jump rope

These girls jump rope in Nepal.

United States

Brazil

England

Kenya

KIDS AROUND THE WORL

Look at this map. Can you match the children in the photos to the countries where they live?

North America

United States

Atlantic Ocean

Equator

Pacific Ocean

Brazil

South America

Compass Rose
North
West — East
South

Afghanistan

Japan

Nepal

Australia

PLAY

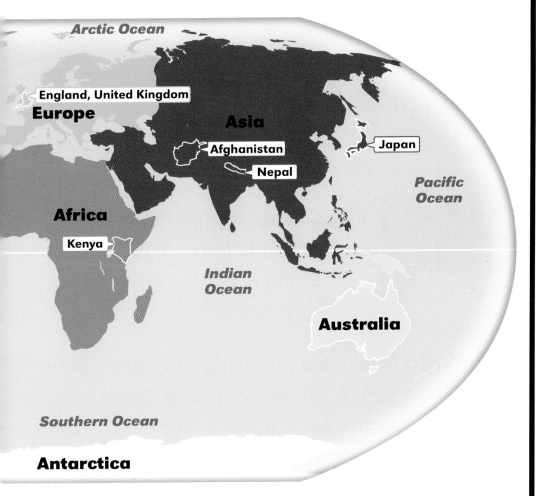

Arctic Ocean

Europe — England, United Kingdom

Asia

Afghanistan

Nepal

Japan

Pacific Ocean

Africa

Kenya

Indian Ocean

Australia

Southern Ocean

Antarctica

YOUR NEW WORDS

bat (bat) a piece of wood used to hit a ball in some sports

jump rope (juhmp rohp) a long rope that a player swings over the head and then jumps over

kites (kites) frames covered in paper or fabric that are attached to a string and fly in the wind

mancala (mahn-**ka**-la) a kind of board game where players move stones or seeds around and capture each other's pieces

marbles (**mar**-buhlz) small colorful glass balls, or the name of a game played with them

soccer ball (**sok**-ur bawl) the ball used in a game where people score by kicking the ball into a goal at the end of the field

tops (tops) toys that spin on a pointed end

INDEX

FIND OUT MORE

Book:

Hollyer, Beatrice. *Wake Up, World! A Day in the Life of Children Around the World.* New York: Henry Holt and Co. BYR, 1999.

Website:

PBS Kids

http://pbskids.org/arthur/games/connectworld/index.html

MEET THE AUTHOR

Amanda Miller is a writer and editor for Scholastic. She and her dog, Henry, live in Brooklyn, New York. Her favorite game is four square.